# The Rough Drafts Series

## Sonnets and other words
## 2022

Tales, Thoughts & Tones

@ Present, Past and Repast

(w/ end-notes)

## Clark Parsons

**Cover Art: Jane Kenyon**

Copyright © 2023 Clark G Parsons

ALL RIGHTS RESERVED. This book contains material protected under International and Federal Copyright Laws and Treaties. Any unauthorized reprint or use of this material is prohibited. No part of this book may be reproduced or transmitted in any form or by any means, electronic or mechanical, including photocopying, recording, or by any information storage and retrieval system without express written permission from the author / publisher.

Paperback ISBN-13: 978-1-952493-27-0

Hardback ISBN-13: 978-1-952493-30-0

Author and Interior Illustrator: Clark G Parsons

Cover image: Jane E. Kenyon

Published:
Jujapa Press, LLC
PO Box 269
Hansville, Wa 98340

NOTE: The views, preferences and opinions expressed by the authors in these pages belong solely to the author and do not necessarily reflect the views, preferences and opinions of Jujapa Press, LLC, or anyone other than the author.

# Dedication

When I look back at my life, the first time I played a father role was when my daughter almost didn't make it from the delivery room. From her inception to today, my love for her had grown and developed as I have grown and developed my capacity for love. When she was but six months old, I made a special carrier for her so she could come with us when we hiked. I took her to piano lessons that were an hour from our home. I helped her with math homework, attended her school events, and later sang with her, her mother and brother in a madrigal group. She helped me create a fake fireplace for a barbershop concert almost ten years ago (see sonnet 22:52). It's still being used. I have always been proud of who she was and that she turned out to be the lovely, talented and resourceful woman she is. She is also a great parent, and although she and I still don't always see eye to eye, we have, whether good or bad, some of the same traits. Well, she may not think so. 😊 So, I dedicate the good parts of the memories that created this book to her. I also thank her for all the joy and pride she has brought to my life, and for my amazing granddaughter.

I also dedicate this book to the therapist who suggested that I try to write some poetry to stir around some of the memories from my past and consider how they may still have an impact on my life today. I doubt she suspected that this book would volley forth from that suggestion. I would not have done this without her suggestion. So, thank you to her.

# Foreword

This collection is a result of a therapy prompt, an optional assignment, from Janis M. that started in late 2021. These sonnets are reflections on things from the past, what happened today (now), and for some days it was non-random silliness.

These collections of words in the Shakespearean sonnet format—I beg Will's forgiveness for any misuse of his form—as a way to force word selection and rhyme where none was originally present.

The ideas and situations presented are reminders of what was racing through my mind and life during the day(s) I wrote each particular piece. Some pieces were finished in one day; others took weeks.

Perhaps some of these expressions will touch the reader who may be dealing with similar issues in their own life.

In an effort to protect the guilty as well as the innocent, names are sparingly used.

I am not a poet, as you will readily see. I dropped the poetry class in my MFA program because I just didn't "get it." My sister still thinks I don't get it, but I've had some introspective fun with this project and plan to continue it as long as I live. I do love to play with words, and since we have the Internet and rhyme finders, it's easier than when a wandering goatherd poet needed to be a master of words.

I have three adult children with whom I played and joked when they were younger. My boys still throw a pun or two around with me, kind of like playing catch or shooting baskets; did that one make it? Did you catch the connection?

Even now, when I look back at last year's offerings, it helps me remember the things I was thinking at the time. Yes, it's essentially a diary, since there are no goals other than to end the year with a sonnet a week.

If one of these seems weird or doesn't have the rhyme or the meter, go on to the next one. I won't be ashamed and neither should you be; this was mostly for me, but if you can get something out of it, welcome!

The text on the next page is a mirror image. You can read it in the mirror or by taking a picture of it with your phone and using the picture editor to flip it over. For instructions, see: flip and image on an iPhone

## Backward

If you would rather work through this backward, go to the N'ed (End) Notes and start there. Read until you find what seems like an interesting topic and go forward and check the related sonnet. Of course, starting around week 28, I added a Haiku and a Limerick with each Sonnet. The Haiku are mostly solemn suggestions, but the Limericks are what they are supposed to be, silly and most-likely ridiculous. Enjoy it, either way!

# Sideward

It might be useful to give you a few clues about the poetry forms used in this book so you don't get sideward about it. Below is one way to understand the three forms: Sonnet, Haiku, Limerick. Each one is a change of pace from the others. Attempting these forms, may not mean success.

**Son-net**: There are several sonnet forms. We use the Shakespearean sonnet form: 14 lines comprised of 3 quatrains (4 lines) following by a couplet (2 lines). In each quatrain, lines 1&3 rhyme, as do lines 2&4. The rhymes do not necessarily carry across all quatrains. The two lines in the couplet rhyme. An additional format provision is that the rhythm (the beat) is iambic pentameter: there are ten syllables per line, with syllables 2,4,6,8,10 emphasized. Sonnets often feature two contrasting characters, events or emotions. Sonnets are often about desire, love.

**Hai-ku**: (High Koo) 3 lines, 17 syllables in the format - 5 in the first line, 7 in the second, 5 in the third. There is no prescriptive rhyme or rhythm. Haiku was originally focused on nature. A Haiku is meant to share, in one breath, a sensory image of a single moment in time.

**Lim-er-ick**: Limericks have five lines; lines 1, 2, 5 are longer and they rhyme. Lines 3, 4 rhyme with each other, and they are shorter. The distinctive limerick rhythm is not always achieved in this book. Limericks are usually funny, even ridiculous, and are meant to elicit a laugh.

# Onward

Now begin the sonnets, haiku and limericks.

Note, again, that I am not a poet but it was suggested that I attempt poetry as therapy, not knowing, of course, what genie would come out of my bottle. Perhaps the stocks would have been better therapy, or dunking or buying the services of a exorcist. But my ordeal, my penance was writing a poem a week during 2022. But in case the demons are still there, and they probably are, I'll be continuing on for 2023 in the book you'll see a year from now if I make it until then.

It's my opinion that crafting correct rhythm and rhyme for a sonnet is not a easy task. I started each one by getting the ideas down first and next getting the meter to work and finally the rhyming pattern. It was a bugger to get the rhymes and you'll notice that sometimes they don't "quite" rhyme. Try to write one yourself to see if it works for you. Write one for a football, a fishing quarry, a playing child, a bouquet of kale, or a flitting butterfly. But don't be alarmed if the words don't fall into place naturally. Enjoy.

# Table of Contents

**Winter Quarter ::: Peak Poke ..........5**

22:01—Flossed .................................................. 7
22:02—Masks .................................................... 8
22:03—Why Masks? ......................................... 9
22:04—My Masks ........................................... 10
22:05—Good Measure ................................... 11
22:06—Stones ................................................. 12
22:07—Rock .................................................... 13
22:08—Cairn ................................................... 14
22:09—Silent Partner .................................... 15
22:10—Double Blessing ................................ 16
22:11—Pain Mongers .................................... 17
22:12—Dueling Menus .................................. 18
22:13—Lexicon ............................................... 19

**Spring Quarter ::: Apple Blossoms ............ 21**

22:14—Trusting .............................................. 23
22:15—A Brighter Smile ............................... 24
22:16—Word Genius ..................................... 25
22:17—Giddy-up ............................................ 26
22:18—Giddy Down ...................................... 27
22:19—CPAP Haps ........................................ 28

22:20—Footsie ........................................................ 29
22:21—PS Magician ............................................. 30
22:22—Thoughts As Nine .................................... 31
22:23—Second Fiddle .......................................... 32
22:24—Paper Trail ............................................... 33
22:25—Sonnets ..................................................... 34
22:26—Cork 'n Chik ............................................ 35
**Summer Quarter ::: Daisy Fields .................... 37**
22:27—Guests ....................................................... 39
22:28—Checks ..................................................... 40
22:29—Therapy .................................................... 41
22:30—30,000 Days ............................................. 42
22:31—Finding Home ......................................... 43
22:32—A Gift ....................................................... 44
22:33—Mobiles .................................................... 45
22:34—Failures .................................................... 46
22:35—Jabber-Clarky .......................................... 47
22:36—Fact-Truth ................................................ 48
22:37—Losing ...................................................... 49
22:38—Warts ........................................................ 50
22:39—Gravity ..................................................... 51
**Fall Quarter ::: Rainbow Gold ........................ 53**
22:40—Single Story ............................................. 55

22:41—What You Know ................................ 56
22:42—Saying No ......................................... 57
22:43—Losing It ........................................... 58
22:44—Be Helpful ........................................ 59
22:45—Be Happy ......................................... 60
22:46—Crastinate ........................................ 61
22:47—Self-reliance .................................... 62
22:48—Not My Fault ................................... 63
22:49—A Nuff .............................................. 64
22:50—Self-reliance Uh-Oh ........................ 65
22:51—Gift Gotcha ..................................... 66
22:52—Faux Fire ......................................... 67
**Not A Quarter ::: End Notes ......................... 69**

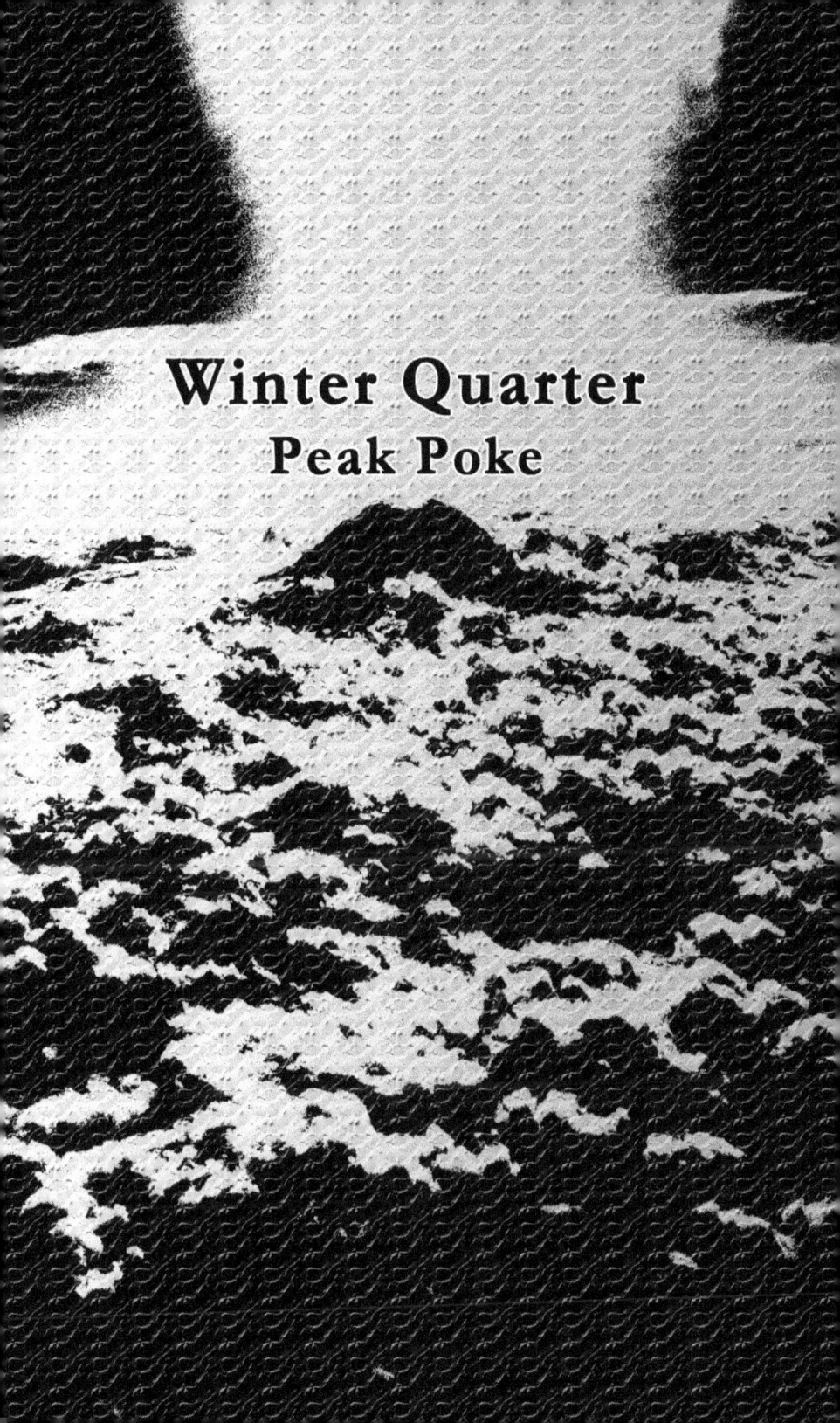

## 22:01—Flossed

It was abrupt, a slap both broad and deep,
Abuse and inconsistency my crime.
Before that day, I had no clue, no peep,
It ripped my soul and left a wound sublime.

I'd left a place so conflict would not sway,
But leaving was the prompt to light the fire.
The claim it was I'd always walked away
When difficulties clouded peace with ire.

Reflecting then upon my past behaves,
I saw a pattern selfish and unkind,
That smelled of caddish lout and senseless raves,
A product of my egocentric mind.

Throughout my life I'd often served my lust,
Though most times thought I'd offered trust.

## 22:02—Masks

So do you know who hides beneath your mask?
Which masks, of theirs, do others wear for you?
And when we share, "Which masks are used?", you ask.
"Does each connect use masks of diff'rent hue?"

Your mask of tease or joke may not show clear
That you bring humor as a positive,
But teasing words can sometimes bring a tear,
Not the uplift that you hoped to give.

Transparent masks, or none, might save the day
If you brought pain when your intent was coy.
And x-ray through their masks might let you stay
And be the friend to play and share a joy.

Nor soulmates, children, moms nor pops can know
What lurks or glows inside that doesn't show.

## 22:03—Why Masks?

Why masks? Do you fear someone knowing you?
The not quite perfect, never good enough,
The you behind the face that fakes what's true,
To hide the guy you think is not so suave or tough?

The girl that isn't cool or cute, she thinks,
But wears rebellious masks to hide her fright.
Or one aloof that shows indifference,
That really hides what she thinks she can't fight.

Someone you know might like you just for you,
But you won't know that possibility.
The mask you wear might make them wear one too.
Removing masks might set you both quite free.

Yes, there are risks by letting your face show;
A set of masks is not the way to go.

## 22:04—My Masks

Why masked? And not my true and lovely self?
It's not so true and lovely, need I say.
A smaller kid, and not just off the shelf.
A nerdy kid, not in the cool set, nay.

I looked for self at home and school and war,
But had the perfect, tougher, goal for dad,
Who was the poor-man's Sweitzer; mask he wore.
Second place was losing. Not first was bad.

Always somewhat shy but aching for a hug,
Not ugly, but not manly and not suave.
I fell with passion but it was a drug,
Still trying, ne'er assuaged; I failed at love.

Ashamed I didn't win, unlovable.
I wear a tragic mask; it's laughable.

## 22:05—Good Measure

And what, my friend, can measure fair a man?
Our movies, books and songs list ways we do.
Is measuring a man distinct from what you'd plan
To use to measure, then, a woman, child or you?

A cup of kindness, add a dollop of cheer,
Then with good intention, stir in fitness and prayer,
With pieces of peace, a worthy vision now clear,
A recipe meant for all folks includes care.

A soupçon of brave might be just what it takes
To brew a skosh, a smidgen-like mug of less fear.
Append a dash, a pinch, a tad of breaks,
Good fortunes flourish; worthy peeps appear.

That boy's a handful, but then two handfuls are ten.
And how do we count up a handful of men?

### 22:06—Stones

Is besting schrunds your boo, or scram-bling scree?
Ascending rocks, like Cruise', all toothy sheer?
You flaunt your stones, and hubris spew with glee?
Are thousand foot drops not reason to macho fear?

I tried that face, just mimicked buddy above.
Knees knocked, brow sweat, launched prayer, no fall my hope.
I vowed safe climbs from then, a life for love.
Deep breaths, stern swear, ne'er again with no rope.

I have no clue why that day was I spared.
Ten ticks of scream, a thud, the end if I fell.
The hand just dealt, was life to help forecast?
Or did destiny die down my ego's deep well?

At four-score plus, few lauds, near final bell,
Done trashed ol' Cruiser's gift, reprieve from hell?

## 22:07—Rock

Is he a rock, or she? How do you know?
If fudging details, they might spice the day,
But on a pledge, it's not the way they go.
If you can always count on them, a rock be they.

Though most rocks are, they didn't start so fine.
Like igneous magma, so nicely hardened outside,
Within precious crystals truly feng shui aligned.
So ready for walkway, wall or to scrape down a hide.

A rock will hold your hand when life gets dark,
Will warm your chilly feet when flames go out.
Can be rock-solid instead of flakey lark,
Will keep you safe and give you ref'rence stout.

Go find your rock to vouchsafe in your heart,
Come water hell or high, rock will not part.

## 22:08—Cairn

A cairn's a force, the wisdom from a heap
Of rocky gems, diverse of size and shape,
Of great variety, with colors broad and deep,
With wisdom from diversity innate.

Count on a cairn to guide your wan-de-ring,
Through dangers, deserts, tough terrain and,
Yes, meadows mild with gently flowing spring,
To nurture, shield and take you by the hand.

A respite for the lost, misguided soul,
To get you back on track and lead your feet
To des-tin-a-tions way beyond your goal,
And get you where your stronger self you meet.

And don't forget a cairn's soul will start
You on the route that tugs inside your heart.

## 22:09—Silent Partner

Have you a spouse, a friend, a brother, sis,
Who shares a room, a place, a morning break,
Who's very much alive by all you guess,
But didn't seem to hear you when you spake?

Is it an aural failure that's the cause,
A stroke, or Alzheimer's that turned the key?
Or could it simply be their focus pause,
To live some dream or bucket fantasy?

Or, did you act-u-al-ly fade from sight
And they, they cannot see you anymore?
Or have you lost your voice, so they have naught
To hear, although you play the narrator?

Or do those hidden iPhone buds in truth
Share expert, real-time nuggets? Ah, forsooth!

## 22:10—Double Blessing

When I was young and oh so very green
I heard the match I thought I ne'er would meet.
A romance chase found me a heart-felt queen;
And soon a loving blessing child's heart beat.

There were some scary moments 'fore the birth,
But baby girl did bless our world soon after.
That tot grew up to read 'bout Suzy's berth
And sang, piano'ed, fiddled to the rafter.

She proudly served the USA for four,
And then was wed, herself, and daughter birthed
Who also garnered pride by mom and pops,
For her big part in adding music, mirth.

Life's twists may not be what you thought they'd be,
But could be also serendipity.

## 22:11—Pain Mongers

Felt pain a therapist has charged you for?
A physical, emotional, an ouch?
You paid for help to lift you from the floor,
And what they gave seemed not a healing touch?

It dredged your tears from pressure so intense
That only dungeon torture is a start.
Count Rugen from the Princess Bride would sense
This hurt will top a Guinness record chart.

What do they teach our therapists, do train,
In all the years of actions and words spoke?
And should it help their clients ease the pain
And not to add the hurting probe and poke?

Aha! It is the pain that brings relief
And saves the day with joy instead of grief.

## 22:12—Dueling Menus

She always made his favorite dining eats.
He never was inclined to "order in."
How could she know that he would love her treats?
A lucky guy he was; each meal a win.

Her entrées never showed a lick of fail.
He praised and thanked her for her foody skill.
Aware she never, ever served him kale,
Her culinary efforts filled the bill.

Yes, he could find the sweet, the sav'ry fill
In any of her offered din din deals.
Yes, she just cooked what seemed to top the hill.
She knew just what he'd treasure for his meals.

He had discriminating taste for sure,
But she knew how to keep up the allure.

## 22:13—Lexicon

An Esperonto[1], Na'vi[1] surely not;
It grows from pairs and groups, a shorthand gram,
Unique to fam, to clique, to gang, this glot
Is understood as meat, as bread, as jam.

It beckons back to common times, a place
Back when your two or few shared claps of time
That captured glimpses in your private space
Inside a word, a phrase, a simple rhyme.

It even passes on ahead to folk
Who were not there, though locals will avow,
And it can grow so newbies do not joke
About a sow who thought she was a cow[2].

And so it seems that kangaroo[3] unplanned
Might be the lex for "do not understand."

---

[1] Both Esperonto and Na'vi are intentionally contrived languages.
[2] The pig/cow story is a local one to rural Poplar, WI.
[3] See Arrival, the movie, to understand this kangaroo.

## 22:14—Trusting

Is there a single soul that you can trust?
A sibling, spouse, a child or closest friend?
And what does it mean for a trust to bust?
How do you know if a trust can mend?

And what about yourselves? The uncle Muns
My mom spoke of? The me, myself, and I?
So do you follow through, hold to the guns
You've set to route your future, your sky pie?

If you can't trust yourself, should others try?
Are you as good's your word, your vow, your drum?
Can others count on you, to never lie?
When push and shove together try to come?

Just like the chicken/egg what's first, what's true?
And can you trust if no-one can trust you?

## 22:15—A Brighter Smile

The heather on the hill in Brigadoon,
The Broadway musical by Learner- Lowe,
A dancing Kelly and Charise, their tune?
Uh, no, but surely pretty, such a pro.

A date with Heather is no cheap affair,
Deep pockets earn deep pocket's spec'al care,
Along with commentary step by step,
Preceded by her numbing drumming flair.

The Heather world is not for faint of means.
And faint of jaw soon learn of her pro plans.
It's soon dudes find a way for extra cleans
So they'll again be cradled in her hands.

The sirens luring Greek Odysseus
Could not out-woo the hygiene queen of us.

## 22:16—Word Genius

Not me, but just a daily email post,
A juicy word which mem'ry cannot ink.
So how do I begin to be a host
For meaty words whene'er I write and think?

Today it is an arneacious[1] gem
And yesterday a reliquary[2] box.
On Monday 'twas ebullient[3], ahem,
Ah, fin'ly one that I can use in talks.

So can you find ebullients to hire
To help your arneacious rocks
Into a reliquary box retire
Without display of weird-ish titup[4] gawks.

Yep, titup was last Sunday's Gen'ius word,
It also was a word I ne'er had heard.

---

[1] Consisting of sand or particles of a substance similar to sand.
[2] A container for holy relics.
[3] Cheerful and full of energy.
[4] Move with jerky or exaggerated movements.

## 22:17—Giddy-up

I did feel giddy Tues-day; very up.
Do up and giddy always stand alone?
Were Western horses urged to "get thee up?"
Or were those ponies urged to reach the zone?

Is feeling giddy same as feeling up?
So could we say, I'm giddy, giddy, yes,
Or is a shorter phrase, I'm up, I'm up.
And giddy-up for mounts alone I guess.

Well, Cosmo, in his Seinfeld sitcom text
He used the giddy-up per his own call
To mean that he was ready for what's next
And equines didn't enter in at all.

So even words we think we clearly know
For others leads them down a diff-rent row.

## 22:18—Giddy Down

If you can giddy-up, what's giddy down?
No more a ref'rence to some riding trails,
But focus on euphoric inner crown.
You know, when goose bumps dot your fingernails

Last week I had my giddy down, I found,
When coach of voice she tweaked my pitch approach,
So I could reach with ease the higher sound.
Well, CPAP may have forged new flow a skosh.

Whate'er it was, my giddy got the drift.
I really had it down. No fluke, real giddy found.
And like the Chord 'twas Lost, I wonder if
In Heaven will I sing again that sound.

So if you've got it down, you'd know you would.
But maybe only time will tell if it's for good

## 22:19—CPAP Haps

What's haps, or what's the haps today? Confess!
I do remember saying, hearing "haps."
'Twas in the nineteen sixties, my best guess.
A ref to happening, the trendy raps.

My "haps" right now a CPAP daily twist
For napping; phone calls to my RRT,
My local Res-pri-tor-y Therapist,
To send sleep data 'til infinity.

Replace the filter and the latex beaks
Each month and do a daily water fill.
And make a sonnet rhyme iambic beats
To yet retain some sanity and skill.

And what's the latest haps with you, my friend?
What contrived nonsense makes your life extend?

## 22:20—Footsie

I have a new excitement in my news.
It's rubbing my wife's feet before she'll bed.
A chance to talk of many things like shoes
And sealing wax is where our words have led.

Not walrus nor a carpenter are there
Inside my office spot, nor oysters, nor
A sandy beach to stroll for secret fare,
Though toes and arch we nightly do adore.

We snack on humor from the day, nor miss
Tomorrow things; and where to put the table top
For rubbing and massage. And then a kiss
Right in the air, a kiss that need not stop.

Now you might think our day end's not so much,
Should talk of love, but we do time-shared touch.

## 22:21—PS Magician

Though PhotoShop's not for the faint of heart,
My younger son he has that PS tamed.
He makes it dance and sing his tune to start
And finish with a glow, a texture framed.

His skill is sought by sculptors, artists all
In need of photos that the world applaud.
This lad did also coach and play fußball
And sang both madrigal, Forever Plaid.

He also boards with wake and snow alike,
And did real dadding for teen girls, a pair,
Whose mom had ring-swapped with this PS tyke,
When deadbeat bio dad was never there.

Hard working, honest, and creative lad,
This charmer does reveal his tricks to dad.

## 22:22—Thoughts As Nine

My weekly soakage in the Hanson stream
Told me go back to when I was but nine,
To think of my full life's desired dream,
And dredge my brain for any mentor sign.

No mentors, save vicar'ous Scouting dad
Who worked so well with his own bio gnome,
Whereas my dad was seldom to be had,
But did provide full table and fine home.

And my life dreams; I found what pages bring
About inventors with creative lean.
I thought that I could build a better thing
If I just knew what that thing would have bean.

'Twas told at school I could be anything,
I still don't know what anything would be.

## 22:23—Second Fiddle

My being second fiddle is the stuff
That eats away at me because my pops
He always said that if it were too tough
For others it was surely right for us.

Although I have my talents and my skill,
My sons and others normally surpass
What I can do or did or might could fill,
If I would put my mind to it, alas.

Indeed I topped them all one time. Above
My grade in math, and yet I got high score
By doing more of easy probs, skipped tough,
And scored above the ones who did know more.

So maybe that's the way to field too tough.
Perhaps an easy way is quite enough.

## 22:24—Paper Trail

I leave a paper trial behind me, it's my cape,
And I don't mean what flushes down the drain.
It is the folded paper, cash, or shape
Like ball, or sampan floating boat, or crane.

The origami squares are in my vest,
And, yes, a fiverr has a pocket home
Until with homeless folk I do invest.
It is part of my living catacomb.

In restaurants, or stores, or waiting room
I sometimes see a lad or lass who's bored;
My flapping bird will often lift their gloom
Or ease the day for those who give them board.

It's good for them, and also good for me.
It surely serves to bring both of us glee.

## 22:25—Sonnets

A sonnet is a weird ol' bunch of lines.
In England, Shakespeare used to write this thing.
Way back in AD 16 hundred times
His pen one hundred fifty-four did bring.

His sonnets have but fourteen lines divine
That are quatrains and couplets, so they say.
And rhythmic beats i-am-bic five per line.
And there's some picky rhyming to display.

Those rigid rhyming rules will never frown
When final sounds of every other line
In a quatrain is like what's two lines down.
In couplets both lines share a final rhyme.

What does it say, when push it comes to shove?
It's naught but to express that thing called love.

## 22:26—Cork 'n Chik

Yon Cork 'n Chik have quite a bag of tricks,
The kids we give our future too, they are!
Inquisitive 'n focused ten and six
They both bring joy; each one a sparkling star.

Oh, they can puzzle with the best of them,
And draw—their art is like an iPhone snap.
They help each other like the best of friends
Would do to free the other from a trap.

They help their mom and dad do daily chores
Like pick up toys, and doing what they can
To tidy up the dishes and the floors.
It's done with joy and to fulfill the plan.

A mom and dad who shield them like a glove;
Mamaw, Papaw who give them all their love.

# Summer Quarter
## Daisy Fields

## 22:27—Guests

Do guests, like fish, begin to smell day three
As Benji Franklin said? Was that a ploy?
We just had four four weeks, I disagree,
But not the fish. There was no smell, much joy.

What are the gifts that guests bring all unplanned?
Of course, one is the love that children ooze
Just in their being who they are first hand,
As joyful, hopping, playing kangaroos.

You learn that what you thought was a routine,
Is not the way that others sanely sculpt
Their cooking, cleaning, eating and between
In spite of how your status quo had skulked.

What we had thought a sane and prudent helm
Was sane and prudent diff'rently for them.

## 22:28—Checks

We humans, as adults or kids, need checks.
'Cause tantrums, crazy ways live on inside
Through time, unbridled might we create wrecks
And do whate'er we please when irked, denied.

The drunk, the shooter, angry child's twitch
Alone to bang a gun, keyboard, make fire
And left alone to freely scratch an itch
May frenzy self to reach new heights of ire.

We kids of ages all can soon abort
The ways we normally deport within
And need a jim'ny cricket of some sort
To curb our urge to rouse the evil twin.

Sometimes a parent or a friend can serve
To keep us straight at times we tend to swerve.


**Haiku**
I can outrage me.
Don't leave me all by myself.
Hold me hand, me back.

**Limerick**
A blaster who came from Tukwillow.
Could disaster himself with a pillow.
If it fell off the bed.
He would tear off his head.
And the steam from his ears it would billow.

## 22:29—Therapy

We're told most therapy is for our good,
It's there to help us when our world, our mind,
Our parts, they are not working as they should.
It is a treatment that may seem unkind.

Unkind, no ma'am, but not a pleasant morn.
Seems that to rid the muscle, mental pain
An effort, not sweet cream, but stingy thorn
Will help the mind and body aches abstain.

And therapy is not a beep-beep fowl
That fools the coy-ote plan and saves the day.
It's more a tortuous tortoise kind of plow,
To get your parts in order for your stay.

If you dare jump for therapy, my friend,
Be prepped to ache; expect a distant end.


**Haiku**
Therapy ain't bliss.
It hurts, ain't fast, you struggle.
There's no guarantee.

**Limerick**
There once was a geezer from Hansville.
Who therapized himself to the fill.
He wrote sonnets late,
Tried to meditate,
And struggles with life even still.

## 22:30—30,000 Days

My 30 K this year, month 9, day 4.
Is this of value? No, it doesn't jive;
It is a nice round number, not much more.
In 2050, 40K arrives.

I don't expect to blow the candles from my bed,
For that's when 40 thousand days arrive.
And it is twenty-seven years ahead
And I'm not sure I'll make it there alive.

There's no time warrant for these bods we hath
We take whate'er we got, change oil and tune;
See doctor, dentist, shrink and natur'path,
And thank the Lord for all the blessings strewn.

If we don't live to reach an age, so what?
We still can lev'rage ev'ry day we've got.


**Haiku**
We have a few days.
Do what you can while you're here.
You'll have some regrets.

**Limerick**
There once was a bloke with no song.
'Cause he didn't want to be wrong.
He would readily poke,
At his neighbor's wrong note,
Though ne'er a right note had he spawn'd.

## 22:31—Finding Home

There is a home inside of us, a balm
To visit when our anger, fear, release
Do overwhelm us and we lose our calm,
That quiet place where everything's at peace.

We need to stock that place before the rage,
Before the moment when we lose our cool,
Before we gravitate to something we'd engage
If we're not in that quiet, sacred pool.

That shelter is our inner home, our safe
Soft teddy we can hold and soothe our ails
Where we regroup and spare the world our strafe
When we have ridden off the rails.

Sometimes we lose our compass when the bear
Pops out to threaten that for which we care.


**Haiku**
Finding your safe spot
When your world has hijacked you
Will save you and it.

**Limerick**
There once was a headstrong young mollusk
Who had lost the map to his solace.
He stuck out his neck
When he should have pulled back
And found that he wasn't so flawless.

## 22:32—A Gift

On many days I wear my loser yoke;
'Twas countered with a simple phrase this week.
"You have a gift," she said. 'Twas unprovoked.
A gift? …and was not said with tongue in cheek.

A gift's a thing that's giv'n, you did not earn.
And if you have one should you aim to share
This skill, this talent, blessing, not spurn
It as a burden you for life must bear?

A teacher and performer, with proud past,
She was the one declared it was a boon.
At least I have one, but it may not last;
Nerve atrophy may nip it 'for I croon.

Do we give thanks for gifts that can't mature?
Or are there none that really stay secure?

**Haiku**
Told I have a gift.
Can I share it 'fore I die?
It's waning; what now?

**Limerick**
There was an old doof with a gift.
Through the options he wanted to sift
As he aged it appeared
The gift waned as he feared.
And his giving was given short shrift.

## 22:33—Mobiles

I demoed to young ladies six and ten
Some seesaw, teeter-totter physics sounds
With words like lever, fulcrum, foot-nuts e'en
Because our weights were truly nuts not pounds.

I pinched small binder clips on dow'ls and took
Some hooks I fashioned from old paper clips.
For dangles found a random measure cup;
Stirred in a swirl of cooking spoons; more drips.

In but a moment they could do their part
To choose new kitchen ware, then balance true
Their version of the ever-changing art,
A task they could not previously do.

As fidgety as balanced art can be,
Was it the teacher or the taught? All three?


**Haiku**
Swirling dervish, not!
Lesson in levers and force.
Hung teeter totters.

**Limerick**
There once was a nut on a limb,
Who had gone with a bolt to the gym.
When his fulcrum he lost
He slipped and he tossed
Yes, their future surely seemed grim.

## 22:34—Failures

Mere few could say they failed as much as I,
In school, in marriage, as a parent, too.
'Though yes, I have kept trying to retry,
And can, indeed, claim some, but not a slew.

So, rarely did I ever make a plea
'cause dad said being tough was our top shelf.
I did not want to 'smurch fam' dignity;
Not be invincible all by myself.

It's true that failing may close doors, but may
In fact will also launch the boat that sails
Us down a diff'rent path where we may nay
Have ever gone before without the fails.

It's not that failing is an ace of spades;
We still will need to make the lemonades.


**Haiku**
Always handle things,
Never ask for any help;
Deluding mantra!

**Limerick**
There was a young man from Kitsap
Who learned from his father this trap.
Too tough for the others
Is just right for us-ers
Yes, he had many a too-tough mishap.

## 22:35—Jabber-Clarky

When I grewvolved*, back then and even wifed,
The voices from my parely*, and inside
They pushed me to no-some where I play life
With rage-mones*, anger and a no-help pride.

With Kermit, it ain't easy being seen
For fail-sess* and for wandrive* with an itch
To be whate'er 'twould be my destinene*,
If I had star a wagon tongue to hitch.

So here am I dis-bobbled and perskew*,
So near the famed dirt blanket to espy,
With still no vorpal* snick my drags to slew
And still in truth not knowing who am I.

'Twere many souls I hurt with my live-Id*,
And but li'l hope to postfix damage did.

*See End-notes 22:35 for dictionary

### Haiku
Nonsensical, yes!
Who I am inside is me.
Someone I don't know.

### Limerick
I once was a Tex or a Doc,
I was called one of these round the clock.
I never was neither,
But answered to either
The real me, of course, not in stock.

## 22:36—Fact-Truth

Sometimes it seems that others lie, they do,
But they contend that it's alternate fact.
My fact is but a fact in science hue,
It's when a switch is on or off, no slack.

But in another realm a fact can mean
What's in the heart , it is the sayer's view,
And not a read-out from a cold machine.
The truth to them may differ from my true.

So, heart truth may diverge from measured word
And so there's no good way to measure truth
If truth is what you saw or felt or heard.
Regardless of the insta-replay booth.

The "whole darn truth and nothing but" is gray.
It may to me be warm; it's cold, you say.


**Haiku**
Is truth simply fact?
Or what's in our heart or head.
Sometimes it's the same.

**Limerick**
There once was a boy, a complainer.
Who cried "wolf" but not 'cause of danger.
He really  was scared,
And wasn't prepared
When the townfolk thought him a feighner.

## 22:37—Losing

Yes, losing can be winning if a win
Will mean you lose your way, your sacred self.
Or if it's more important for another one to gin,
Then beat the odds and play it for your health.

You may be mocked for winning if it seemed
You won more than your share, though it was chance,
That is, pure luck, and skill was not convened.
So why is it a curse to draw the better stance?

If luck is seldom great when gold's the prize,
But ne'er you got your spouse and kids through graft.
If so, I'd call your fortune greater than
Someone who won at lotto or the draft.

And, yes, the genes, the place, they hedged the bet
But maybe luck stood nearby when you met.


**Haiku**
Losing's relative.
The game's played for the long term.
Plan to win later.

**Limerick**
There once was a plucky young gamer.
Who wasn't so much an exclaimer.
He played close to the vest,
Never squandered his nest,
And quietly filled his container.

## 22:38—Warts

I have a friend who's full of love and skill
And gives me status as a high ranked pal.
We laugh and cry and share life's daily thrill
And we'll be there high flood or low morale.

And yet, that lady has a snobbish twist,
And seems to peer down her long nose, tut, tut,
About my warts, or how I hold my wrist
With disregard for how her comments cut.

No doubt I could improve upon my mane,
On tidbits 'bout the way I look or think.
It hurts that who I am seems less germane,
Than how I preen or if I lift my pink.

But does the sentence always fit the crime.
Or, oops, am I that snob some of the time?


**Haiku**
Our warts are our quirks.
Friends see them but love us still
Do we act the same?.

**Limerick**
There once was a quirky ol' geezer.
Who kept his hank' in the freezer.
It was used for a cold,
Freeze kept the germs on hold,
And, no, he wasn't a serial sneezer.

## 22:39—Gravity

Sometimes the chips indeed fall where they may
And due to nothing you have thought or done
Or, maybe 'cause of what you think or say.
There's chance those falling chips incite someone.

And other times the chips don't fall, they stay,
They cling, adhere, when rocky crag impose
And you don't fall a thousand feet to splay
Upon the granite lumps of Cruiser's toes.

I have a date with those phalanges, yes.
The fickle fates they stand me up, they play.
It does incite my lips to pray, not stress,
To ponder why I'd lived another day.

When there are times we really need some hope,
There's something to be said for a top rope.


**Haiku**
It's not gravity.
It's not a law of physics
If it falls, I curse.

**Limerick**
I found an old whimpering coot,.
Who declared his motley life was ruint.
A pillow had fallen,
And he sat there bawln'
'Cause the action it wasn't his trut'.

# Fall Quarter
# Rainbow Gold

## 22:40—Single Story

My story came from fam'ly, folks and kin
'Twas all I knew, my childhood point of view
'Twas surely then a good place to begin
And yet it was a route that points askew.

Despite its pretext 'twas by system weighed
With bias gender, race, and attitude.
No grand and evil plan, just swayed
More difficult for some the paths we've hewed.

So what we do not know can bruise, can prank,
Not aimed to hurt, when we choose pedigree,
An undeserving other who has rank
Nor skills nor kindness nor integrity.

Beware your single story when you judge,
Your view may be the one that has the smudge.


**Haiku**
Our single story.
It's what we know, understand.
It's our errant truth.


**Limerick**
There once was a man who knew truth.
He'd known what it was since his youth.
He ate just the rind
From the fruit he could find.
So never vile juice touched his tooth.

## 22:41—What You Know

I heard he'd said that I was old, and slow.
So did he think that I had passed my prime?
And that I could not think or steer the row?
That they should meld a younger clime?

I did not ask him why he'd cut me so,
But took to plan revenge by steady pace.
Like finding ways to sabotage his flow,
But making sure in ways he'd never trace.

Why did he hate me so, say such a thing?
It took me time, and stealth; the ruse was slow.
No matter. Now, I've shown him who is king.
With righteous smirk, I shared he'd been let go.

And he repeats as he descends to go,
He'd ever praise my slow and mindful show.


**Haiku**
They heard you say it.
They knew what you were thinking?
Can they read your mind?


**Limerick**
I once knew a flibberdy-gibbit.
Who knew what you thought 'fore you think it.
He used that great skill
With manure to fill
Up his "life with an alien" exhibit.

## 22:42—Saying No

To be forgiving, walk the second mile
Is great until they want the third or mo'.
At some point you are stretched beyond your smile
And then you, maybe, might just need a "no."

I booked a task about a year ago,
It was to take a month at most to end.
But many waits and alterations flow
And seemed that task to join forever trend.

Just when is it do we a parity exceed?
This task it isn't for a sib time spent
Or boss, a friend, or charity indeed.
How many times is it we should relent?

It's seventy times seven for a slight
But what's an unthanked, endless favor's plight?

**Haiku**
To forgive is good.
Kissing a hinny is not.
Sometimes no's the word.

**Limerick**
I once asked a dad 'bout forgiveness.
Was it seventy times seven or less?
"Turn over your cheek
But don't be a freak
We're not to be shoe mats," he stress'd.

## 22:43—Losing It

Just how did "lose it" visit me today,
And not in person but to type reply?
Yes, anger raged, I don't know what to say.
Ashamed. Wish I could whisk those words goodbye.

It was frustration with a someone, who
Had claimed much expertise with just the skill
I had been asked to do, but would not do
Herself, yet sniped at how I tried to fill.

And all along posed entry level quiz
About what she was surely not a dunce.
And threw "insider" words straight from her biz.
I had withdrawn my offer more than once.

I had come back to help but flashed my "tilt."
Yes, I had felt abus-ed to the hilt.


**Haiku**
Temper your hot spots.
It's patience only while it lasts.
Can't unburn what's ash.

**Limerick**
There once was a snarly ol' termagant.
Who shared room with the proverbial elephant.
He raved when he lost
He turned and he tossed
And the words that he threw were not eloquent.

## 22:44—Be Helpful

You drive that extra mile to help a stiff?
Someone you'd never even seen before?
Someone, today, who may have flipped you off?
Or yet, a him who ridiculed your score?

You volunteer to help a filly, foal
Who struggles with a thing you find passé?
But they do need that skill to reach their goal.
And, yes, you serve that morsel without pay?

But can you find the guts to ask for help
When all your expertise has hit the wall
And now you have the knowledge of a whelp
And show buck naked in the mirror ball.

You use "rad" juices when you give a hand.
To ask for help, it grows the friend of man.


**Haiku**
Help: four letter word
Will I get it when needed?
Might, if I gave it.

**Limerick**
There once was a selfish young tooter
Who thought the world worshipped his scooter.
When he fell down and cried
No one rushed to his side;
Too often he'd called each a loser.

## 22:45—Be Happy

I often hum or sing in line to ship
A package small or large or to rework
A postal item got by 'livry slip.
"Why are you ever happy?" asks the clerk.

Today I sang the birthday tune for sure,
To bagger Marilyn, and she did glow,
When I, indeed, was at the groc'ry store
And checker Brenda told me it was so.

And at the coffee shop I spied a lad
Of three with relatives of him to herd
And promptly grabbed my ready pad
And folded him a flapping 'gami bird.

So why not celebrate and be alive
When being so doth bubble from inside.


**Haiku**
Happy's not frosting.
It just comes from deep inside.
It o'er takes the cake.

**Limerick**
If you e'er encounter a geezer
Who flinches when op'ning the freezer,
You can rest assured
His shake's not absurd
He imagines himself a stripteaser.

## 22:46—Crastinate

Back years ago, put off was crastinate.
No, not with pro prefix we have today.
Could we today invent con-crastinate
To mean we choose instead to not delay!

Con-crastinate, is not conquistador
Although they sought their goals with pluck.
It's also simply not tooth fairy lore
Although some things get done with random luck.

It's best to crastinate with con prefix
And get it done right out the bloomin' gate
So when the car won't start or plays some tricks,
You'll have deliv-er-y and won't be late.

Yes, many times the clock won't do you in.
But, won't an early finish help you win?


**Haiku (satire)**
Gather wood later,
Frolic now in the sunshine.
Climate collapse warms.

**Limerick**
There once was a crass crastintor
Who poo-pooed her deal with Sir Gator
Mr. Croc was incensed
And spurned her defense,
And quickly resolved it; he ate her.

## 22:47—Self-reliance

If it's too tough for all the crowd to face,
Was told by dad 'twas surely right for me.
To ask for help, I'd failed, it was disgrace,
No, I could do it on my own, no we.

And many times in life I made boo boo
But never asked for help or even made
A visit to the prof, or expert to
Get insight 'nough to help me make the grade.

And still today I tend to shy away
From him whose hand is reaching out to me
In gracious human kindness if I stray.
A lunkhead I, though smart 'bout much I see.

So beat me with a truth and I'll comply
Unless my daddy's ghost o'erpowers my try.


**Haiku**
Praise self-reliance.
It's good to make it alone.
Know when to seek help.

**Limerick**
There once was a proud self-reliant.
Who to offers of help was defiant.
He climbed to great height
And swam with his might
But to back massage was compliant.

## 22:48—Not My Fault

So many things I've tried and tried and failed,
And often tried again, and didn't make the grade..
But mostly 'twas the case that when I sailed
That sea again just one more time it paid.

I just found out that one thing I did try
But failed to win, the fault I did not own.
In fact I could not climb to quartet high
Because I could but rarely hear the overtone.

So try's I might I did not have the skill
Because my auditory tools were nix .
So fault it was not me, nor was it lack of will.
Not even hearing aids could do a fix.

So, yes, it's not my fault occasion'ly
When no amount of work brings victory.


**Haiku**
Sometimes it is true
No matter your drive or skill.
Your square peg won't fit.

**Limerick**
There once was a very good singer.
Yet for him overtones did not linger.
He at last knew the score
'Twas the C-130 roar
Wouldn't let him with high pitches tinker.

## 22:49—A Nuff

A nuff is not your fuzzy tribble guest,
Not like the ones on Star Trek stuffing rooms
Nor e'en your pets own squeaky chewy quest
To romp and fetch with you when boredom looms.

A nuff 's enough in actuality.
Is what you are e'en when you've missed a cue.
Or aren't the best, not someone's cup of tea.
You are a nuff and just because you're you.

So when you do your job and try your best
There is no shame in being second place
Or third or fourth, just staying with the rest.
Just being you oft means you've won your race.

There's nothing wrong with having the "right stuff,"
But being friendly, kindly you is quite a-nuff.


**Haiku**
Enough, did she say?
Don't need skills, talents, just me?.
What about winning?

**Limerick**
There once was a young nuff, a noodle.
Who thought he would tie up a poodle.
He wrapped up the paws
And munched with his jaws
But then wished he'd been born a strudel.

## 22:50—Self-reliance Uh-Oh

It's not Ralph Waldo's words you might expect.
I warn, indeed, of too much self-reliance,
That inbred voice that leads you to reject
The mate you might just need on your gridirons.

If it's too tough, accept some little aides.
Sometimes if you do stumble or you fall
And know your comrades might be there in spades.
As you were there to help them mount their wall.

You were happy when you gave your sway
So why not let someone be happy too!
If they can lift or carry you someday.
Turn-about's fair play applies to you.

It's fine to handle most things on your own,
But sharing loads can yield a happier home.


**Haiku**
I go it alone.
Don't need no stinkin' assist.
Even if I'll lose.

**Limerick**
A self-sufficient bloke he did yell "wait"
When his car was rolling fast t'ward the lake.
He never needed help
Even when the kelp
Had filled his car from far below the wake.

## 22:51—Gift Gotcha

So after hours of plans and beaucoup bucks,
Arranging, researching, car miles to boot
Your super fine gift is prepared and with luck
You'll blow the mind of the "To" with this loot.

An ultra-secret gift, Saint Nick's the "From".
Was almost missed, the label used weird font.
It took a hint to get a friend to come,
There stashed neath branches, e'en tho wrapped elegant.

A plain generic box, a throw away?
While wrapped 'twas naught to treasure from afar,
An elephant, for holiday array?
Or eas'ly left behind in nearby bar?

The best laid plans for special gift sent.
Doubt there's much glow from new recipient.


**Haiku**
Anonymous gift.
Although 'tis a great surprise,
Cheats "to" of thanking.

**Limerick**
A senior created a gift that was spiffy
But wrote that it was Santa who's gifty
It was quite a surprise
But the "to" wasn't wise
  'bout to whom she could tell it was nifty.

## 22:52—Faux Fire

A faux shell fireplace, silk flames to flare,
A set addition, stocking hanging space.
And yet, a real connect for dad and heir
While building this symbolic Santa place.

As years go by the set stays good to go,
And yet the fire tween heir and dad, it's true,
Has now become the flame that's partly faux.
With much regret from heir and father, too.

So, when is fire faux and when's it live?
How does it show, and when then can we know
To bellows sparks while life still does abide
Before the ember's cold and without glow.

How can we know when fire is growing faux
Yet we can still restore the heat forged long ago?


**Haiku**
Faux fire ignites
Mem'ries, regrets and options.
Flee, fire, faux, fumble.

**Limerick**
If you were ever a flickering fire
Either faux or a real burning pyre,
With a flame made of silk
Or of a much warmer ilk,
You can e'er be a thing to inspire.

## 22:01—Flossed

This sonnet is a strong reaction, perhaps a little overdone, to the request from someone who had been dear to me for over 50 years to not contact them any longer. This started me on a journey of therapy, weekly meditation, pursuit of Rick Hanson sessions, and eventually the penance of writing a sonnet a week. The sonnets help me reflect on what happened and still happens, at least to some degree, in my relationships to others. I have a lot of regrets and, of course, I can't change the past, but I can try to be a better, kinder, less selfish me as my life continues. Floss gets the junk out from beneath the good parts.

## 22:02—Masks

The supposition here is that we all, at least to some degree, hide who we really are, what we really think, so we can be accepted in whatever current social situation we are in, whether with family, friends, work associates, or other one-on-one interactions, either romantically or formally. We tend to hide, at least I do, what we are and what we aren't. When we look at someone else we see his or her mask, often not the real person inside.

## 22:03—Why Masks?

This is a continuation of 22:02, really. We go to extremes sometimes to hide fear, affection, anger, and a dozen other emotions because they might not be PC (politically correct) or acceptable. Wouldn't it be great to have a someone in your life who knows the real you and likes you anyway?

## 22:04—My Masks

This another continuation of 22:02 but getting personal with me and my masks. I was a good student, a good "soldier" (really), but was never—it seemed—good enough for my father. I imagine his intention was to urge me to do better, but sometimes that was not easy. So a lot of my life was spent trying to be more than I am, even though I am pretty okay in a lot of ways. I never got to be what I thought I should be, but I never even knew and still don't know what I should have become. There's still some time but, sadly, I don't know the destination, yet.

## 22:05—Good Measure
This one mostly plays with folksy measurements but touches on how we appraise (measure) others, even ourselves.

## 22:06—Stones
Do you have the "stones" sometimes refers to having the testicles, the guts, the daring to do something risky or possibly embarrassing. This refers to a real rock climb and real danger and real stupidity that could have cost me my life. I was in my early 20s. To this day, I wonder why I was "allowed" to survive. I also wonder, that if I was spared, what was I supposed to with these 60 years that followed that would have "really" made a difference. Yes, I had 3 great kids, wrote a couple books, and earned a couple advanced degrees. However, I also failed at marriage more than once, and apparently failed with one of my children. What is my contribution; what should it have been? What could it have been?

## 22:07—Rock
This is essentially an ode to a son of mine who wanted to be called "Rock" one year when he was in elementary school. That faded, but once he was away and married, I referred to him that way, and he seemed to take a shine to it, at least he's not told me to "cease and desist." Someone who's a rock is solid and unswerving. Rocks start out amorphous and life shapes them. Some rocks are gems; some give you shelter; some become famous figures.

## 22:08—Cairn
This refers to my older son's spouse. She is likened to a cairn, which is a pun with her name. A cairn is used in the wilderness to guide our way. She did that with students for years and she still has that impact on people, at least she does on me.

## 22:09—Silent Partner
If you ever spend time around someone who is always on the phone either talking or listening to music, or playing video games or watching TV or even reading or in any way absorbed in what they are doing so that they don't hear when you ask a question or make a comment, then that's what a silent partner is. I found out, to my chagrin, that my partner was actually doing things related to her business efforts when she didn't hear me. Of course, I'm sure I've been distracted and not heard her, too. My original thought was that if someone is in the same room with you that they should be able to respond to you. Well, there's a good reason that sometimes that is not the case. ☺

## 22:10—Double Blessing
Just because a child is not planned, per se, doesn't mean they aren't loved and appreciated like one that was sort-of "planned," since it's never a sure thing, and all the stars need to align, etc.. She is talented, resourceful, smart and giving. In fact, that child gave us a delightful and talented grandchild, which made it a double blessing. Still no triple blessing...yet.

## 22:11—Pain Mongers
There are a number of caregivers who help us combat all sorts of issues with teeth, bones, joints, muscles, nerves, as well as with mental and emotional challenges. Seems like there is a little discomfort or pain involved with any of those relief providers. What prompted this sonnet was the Physical Therapist who put pressure on some trigger points along my spine. Yes, it hurt, but when she released the pressure, the soreness along the spine was much relieved. The same would apply to a masseuse or to yourself during your stretching routines.

## 22:12—Dueling Menus
Mealtime is great around our house because I like everything my spouse prepares, and she always prepares things I like. Seems like two ways to say the same thing, but no. Yes, she knows what I don't

like and doesn't serve me Kale, even when she fixes it for herself. But she knows I'll eat and like most any left-over, frozen and reheated, or the second day. A few things actually seem better to me the second day. After more than 25 years, she knows what I prefer, but also knows I will eat most anything she wants to eat. So, the menus don't really duel.

### 22:13—Lexicon
Knowing what someone is saying takes more than knowing the dictionary definition of words they use. There are, of course, dozens and dozens of languages on our planet, but also dozens of local varieties of slang used within a country. Being called "darling" or "hon" by a waitress I'd never seen before did catch my attention, until she used it with every other guy and gal she served. There are also local trivia and folklore that is referenced at times when a newbie or visitor would not comprehend what was meant by what was said. There's the "otter" guy, the "painter," the "computer guy" that we locals know but a visitor wouldn't.

### 22:14—Trusting
Trusting goes both ways, and we need to know if we can even trust ourselves, our instincts, or pledges. Trusting you is important to someone else and trusting them is important to you. We also simply need to know if we will "really" keep our promises and not make them if we can't keep them.

### 22:15—A Brighter Smile
Sitting in a dental chair every four or six months for a hygienist to clean off the tartar and plaque is not an odious task, but hygienists are not all the same. I met my second wife in a dental chair, but since then hygienists have not been the same. My previous hygienist was a man, did a great job. But my most recent is a cut above most others. She was willing to explain why she did each thing, where she got her training, and even explained all about "deep pockets" between the gum and the tooth, and even set up a signal with me to

use if I needed her to stop for me to sneeze or cough or scratch my nose. Yes, she got an A.

### 22:16—Word Genius
For a while, I got a Word Genius message, sometimes two, in my email inbox every day. I typically glance at those words. Some of them I know, but many are never normally used in any conversation I've been included in. In adjacent days this week were three words I'd never heard and one I have enjoyed using. Those three I will probably never use again, but I'll know that I've seen them already, if that is worth anything.

### 22:17—Giddy-up
I got a little giddy after my voice lesson this week, because I had learned an easier and better way to sing the head-tones near the top of my vocal range. What goes with giddy? Giddy up! So giddy and up because the core of this sonnet connects to urging a horse to get a move on. And, of course, dear Kramer used that word/phrase regularly on the Seinfeld show when he was ready to move on.

### 22:18—Giddy Down
If we have a giddy-up, there must be a giddy-down, right? So once you really know how to get giddy, you've got your giddy down, as they say. I had found my "giddy," one I guess I had been looking for, like the organ player looked for the Lost Chord.

### 22:19—CPAP Haps
Learning to use the CPAP is the topic here. The "haps" was a phrase from the 60s meaning "what was going on." CPAP and haps had a similar sound so they bonded together for this sonnet.

### 22:20—Footsie
For the past few months I've been rubbing/massaging my spouse's feet most nights right before she goes to bed. She comes into my office, plops down in the recliner, slides her feet out of her slippers, and sticks her feet up on my lap. I massage her feet and lower legs, as well as separate and pull on each toe (because she wants me to).

We wrap up the day with "the high point of the day" for each of us. She heads to bed, and I continue at the computer or work on music until it's time for me to connect with the CPAP device for the night.

## 22:21—PS Magician
PS stands for Photoshop, a computer program to edit pictures of all sorts. My son is a photographer and uses PS regularly to crop, darken or lighten images or parts of images. He's been doing this for over 30 years and is an expert at it. He also is a singer, wakeboarder—even at age 50, and adopted his wife's kids. I'm proud of this guy; he's a good man.

## 22:22—Thoughts As Nine
This was a prompt from Rick Hanson, an author and online therapist, who asked us to write about what we had planned for our lives at age nine, and also who mentored us at age nine. My dad was a hard worker and provided a nice home; I never went hungry nor lacked for sturdy and serviceable clothes. My parents even sent me to summer camp. However, my dad, himself, was not much for extra-curricular activities.

At school I was told I could do or be anything, which could never be true for anyone, but I didn't know any better. I think my parents tried, but I think I never learned some basic things, like how to study, how to deal with adversity, how to be happy being myself. My thoughts at nine were quite naïve, I think, and I really had no mentors. I admired the dads of other guys who spent time with them and taught them skills. My mom and dad both had lots of "skills," but they never really helped me learn them. I was exposed to them, by example, but never learned them myself. I was not very well prepared for adult life, although I can iron my shirt just fine.

## 22:23—Second Fiddle
Yes, I still have memories of failing, of not being the best, or of regrets that I didn't know enough to be better. However, I do have one memory of a time when I was not the best but outdid others who were more educated and had greater specific skills.. In other

words, if I do the best I can with what I have/know, that is enough. And sometimes it results in a better outcome than from those who knew more.

### 22:24—Paper Trail
This starts with a bit of silliness, but that's integral to who I am. The main point is that I do things for others; I even plan ahead to be ready to do things for others. The paper trail is typically defined as "documents (such as financial records) from which a person's actions may be traced or opinions learned." This paper trail shows my intentions related to reaching out to people.

### 22:25—Sonnets
Yes, this is an instructional piece about writing sonnets, and the rules you must follow to end up with a Shakespearean sonnet. Of course, it doesn't tell the subject matter, even though it suggests that love is to be the intention of a sonnet.

### 22:26—Cork 'n Chik
Cork is the codename for Cora K (age 6), and Chik for Chiara K (age 10). They, along with their parents, were guests at our house for a month in 2022 from mid-May to mid-June. The girls and I spent time folding origami and Moravian Christmas stars. They are sweet kids, well mannered, and helpful.

### 22:27—Guests
This one started out as a concern about long-stay (multiple weeks) guests making life difficult because they had different habits than my wife and I. By the time I got half through with the sonnet, I realized that the positive message is that they have a system that works for themselves, and we have one that works for us. We probably couldn't immediately be effective using their system or them ours. However, it pays to notice what works for them and how we might adopt some aspects of it that we hadn't thought of before.

=== From here, I added a haiku and limerick to the Sonnet. ===
=== They are on the same topic but give a different view. ===

## 22:28—Checks
Following the school shooting in Texas that killed 19 children, I was distinctly reminded that we all need a buffer, a voice, a guide to keep us from getting "too" angry, so angry that we do things we can't control and that we can't apologize away afterwards.

## 22:29—Therapy
These sonnets are an extension of the therapy I've been engaged in for the past eight months. Every day I revisit something from my past and my present as well as consider how I might be different in the future. In addition to the actual sessions with a therapist, I attend several zoom sessions each week, especially with Rick Hanson but also with others, to visit how I interact with others and with myself. As I can, I write about these discoveries in these sonnets. The quality of the sonnets may not be Shakespearean, but they are a diary for me, so I can look back to see what I was thinking during this year or years of contemplation.

## 22:30—30,000 Days
This is mostly a silly reflection on the fact that in a month and a half I will have lived 30,000 days. That's merely a random round number that has no intrinsic meaning unless we give one to it. It is a badge of passing, of living, of making mistakes. I don't expect to get to 40,000 days of living, but I could, and during all those next 10,000 days I hope to be more reflective and more consistently useful and loving than I have been for the first 30,000.

## 22:31—Finding Home
This is a direct reflection on a Rick Hanson lesson. He said in times of frustration or pain or anger we need to know we have a quiet, safe place to go. This place is "home," a figurative home to be sure, but that place inside us where we can soothe the challenges of the day so we don't lose control, lose our heads, even "when all about

us are losing theirs." (Rudyard Kipling). This sonnet shakes hands with 22:28—Checks.

## 22:32—A Gift
My voice teacher told me this Spring that I had a gift. I can still do something with that gift, but my voice was just diagnosed as having nerve atrophy, so I won't be able to grow it like I might have done years ago. That's a kind of sad aspect of our lives when we find out "maybe too late" that we could have done something if we had known and started to grow a gift when we were younger. I don't know exactly what she means, but certainly not the seed of a Caruso, a Bocelli, a Pavarotti, or one of those, but maybe could have made a respectable contribution with the right coaching. Yes, I've been told that I had a nice voice, but never that it was a "gift." We all have gifts of different kinds, some lesser, some greater, but the point is that if we have a gift it would be nice to know so we can choose, or not, to do something with it. Of course, the even greater gotcha is having the dedication to make something with that gift once we know what it is.

## 22:33—Mobiles
A family of four was staying with us for a month. Their two girls, ages 6 and 10, enjoyed spending time with me parts of each day doing puzzles, origami and other paper folding, and watching Disney channel. I got scooters for each of them, a bike for the older one, and put together a make-shift corn-hole game for them. Their father wanted to tell them about writing sonnets, and about making mobiles. I gave him a lesson plan about sonnets, so I put together a Master Mobile kit with which they could learn about levers, force, and how a teeter totter is like the upside down layer of a mobile. In a few minutes they had created a mobile using kitchen utensils.

## 22:34—Failures
One of my father's pieces of advice was that "if it was too tough for anyone else, it was just right for a "Parsons." Of course, that was a prelude to many failures. Some of those were because I was never

taught and never learned how to do things like ask for help or use dependable study skills. So I failed in school, in jobs, and in marriage. I also succeeded in school, jobs and marriages, at least for a while. The other side of failures is that it sends us down a different path; that is, there always seem to be new paths available. I failed at one degree but earned a different one. I failed at one marriage but have had one, now, for 28 years. I look back at what might have happened had I succeeded in one or two of the places I failed; my entire life would have been different, not necessarily better. At times I have been lazy and selfish, and there were many times I failed to ask for the help that might have avoided the failure.

### 22:35—Jabber Clarky
Of course, this was inspired by the Lewis Carroll poem, "Jabberwocky." Word nonsense is part of me, and so charging into this one was a lot of fun. It does, however, dig into my anger issues and not knowing what I should do with my life or who I really am.

grewvolved: grew + evolved
parely: parents + family
rage-mones: raging hormones
fail-sess: failures + successes
wandrive: wander lust + drive
destinene: perversion of destiny so it rhymes with seen
perskew: perverted + askew
vorpal snick: sword and slashing from Jabberwocky
live-Id: living to serve my Id
postfix: fixing after some damage happened

### 22:36—Fact-Truth
Fact is not always equivalent to your own truth since we all see/feel things differently. To you it's cold, to me it's cool, to someone who always lives in cold it might be warm. To some, their perception of easy is not my easy, nor my difficult someone else's difficult. No one else can know how you "actually" feel, how you react inside to some sight, sound, sensation or mental effort. This also leaves others to mis-understand our interpretation of a situation because

their interpretation is different. Now, facts, at least the way I see them, have no room for interpretation. If the meter measured something then we have a fact, at least according to that meter. But we may define a "thing" differently from someone else depending on our measuring equipment. Athletes sometimes find ways to do what seems impossible, like throw or kick a ball that curves.

### 22:37—Losing
Winning is a relative word. Its truth is different. Some think gold, beauty, fame or prestige is winning. Others might consider their faith, relationships or charitable pursuits more valuable. If you lose in an honest wager but the winner gets what they want and you are left with your friends and family and pride, who loses? Some folks seem to win gambles at a higher rate than others do. If you win a winter jacket to add to the ones you already have, but the homeless person doesn't even have a ticket in the game, who wins and who loses? This idea of losing, in this way, refers to a greater good for the whole, not only for yourself. At least that is one way to look at it. And sometimes winning might take us away from the things that really matter most, although we don't realize it at the time.

### 22:38—Warts
I wrote this 2 ½ months ago and no longer remember who that friend was who tended towards honoring superficial features over features of the heart/soul. It's interesting that I thought of her as a good friend, even though she was very picky about stature and wardrobe and my coif. Most of us surely have aspects of who we are that we try to hide from others. Maybe it's that we can't dance, or are overweight, or we're too this to too that. Apparently, this friend I was talking about disregards those "warts" when friendship is on the line, but still has some strong feelings about certain things. I like that. I wish I knew who she was. ☺

### 22:39—Gravity
This is basically about a rock-climbing incident when I was in my early twenties. I didn't fall but was scared enough that I wonder why

I was spared. For some great contribution? No. That didn't happen. In fact, I have failed at many pursuits and relationships. Yet, I think back and wonder why I was spared. Maybe to write this? Mt Cruiser didn't win that day, or did she?

## 22:40—Single Story
Most of us are raised inside one culture, one family's approach to life, one community's sense of worth. That means we bring along the prejudice and bias from that single back-story. So, today we might frame our opinions based on that back-story. Were you raised in a logger family who cut trees for a living, knowing you were helping to make materials to build homes with, or in one that studied the effects of trees in our world related to chemical and physical benefits that disappear when forests are clear cut? Often, we don't even realize we have biases, even ones we are unaware of, just because of where we came from, who raised us, and how that culture planted seeds of "the right way" in our heads. It's indeed difficult to ferret out those biases we don't know we have, to look at situations from the point of view of someone else who has their own biases they aren't aware of.

## 22:41—What You Know
Sometimes we don't "really" know what someone is doing or thinking and make decisions based on faulty intuition. And they may be misreading our actions or lack of actions. Sometimes we think things are going along OK, but for 50 years someone has resented us, feared us, loved us without us knowing, and without us being able to discuss it or deal openly with it. Sure, maybe we do that, too, and if we do, how can the other person or persons repair the bridges. How can you repair bridges if you didn't know the steel bridge you were traveling was but a shaky rope bridge to them. I don't have an answer to this but have become more aware of it recently. And, even if we know there is a long-held issue, how do we approach it quietly and considerately? We humans are quite a challenge.

## 22:42—Saying No

I had a recent experience with saying no, and not sticking with it. At some point, when connections get strained and you can't seem to resolve them, doing more business or favors for someone may need to be halted. That task dragged on and on and the "client," if you will, kept telling me how they had years of experience doing what I was going to help them with. Well, I finally told them I was backing out, and since no contract had been signed, no money had exchanged hands, and no one's life was at risk, I told them they should just do it and I was dropping their request. Seemed like when I started doing something that I was repeatedly reminded that they knew how to do this task, that they had had years of experience with it. I was, honestly, fed up with being told how to do my part of the task, so I gave it back to them.

That lasted about a week and they got back with me and "begged" me to do their task. I agreed, but immediately they came back that they had experience with what I was doing and they used to do "X" and they used to "Y." I would have been better off to hold firm on the "no," and reduce my stress. Eventually, I let their repeatedly reminding me of their "vast experience" with the task push me to anger and I exited the project with hard feelings on both sides, including me being embarrassed for losing my cool. So, if you come to a well-processed "no," think twice about going back to "yes." And the sense of the limerick came straight from my dad's lips.

## 22:43—Losing It

This one relates directly to 21:42, "Saying No." I had said no but had reneged, and at their begging, I had come back to do the job. I had spent a number of hours of computer work on their project, but they kept wanting changes and brought up their history again, and I lost it. It didn't help that the project had been started and then they delayed it for six months. This project dragged on for a year. So, I did work that will never be used. I even sent a thumb drive with my files and it was returned "rejected." Well, that was just spite on their part, but obviously they were upset. I'm sorry that it didn't work out. I'm sorry that I lost my cool, and I wish I would have stuck with my original "No!" I was still honorable at that point, at least I felt I had been. I hope they finish it alone or with someone else, but I didn't' have the patience and negotiating skill to handle that one. Mark one for the yucky part of me. ☹

## 22:44—Be helpful

This is a multi-sided coin. We should be helpful, but should also allow ourselves to ask for help when needed. But we should not "force" our help on others. Most of my life I have pushed help away, knowing "I could do it myself." That "knowing" was and is false, at least untrue. I didn't make it through a number of challenges in my life because I figured if I worked long enough and hard enough, I could figure it out "myself." My dad had a motto: "If it's too tough for everybody else, it's just right for a Parsons." That has served me well sometimes, but not at other times. Knowing when to keep trying and when to ask for help is the tricky part. However, there is some other wisdom from my dad: "No matter how strong you get, you'll never be as strong as an elephant." So that one clashes a bit with the "too tough for everyone else" motto. Now that we have online help about almost anything, it's easier to find help without the world knowing. And "Siri" is helpful in getting that help for us.

And another aspect of help that's important, too, is doing your part to support whatever collective you belong to: family, club, city, state, country.

## 22:45—Be Happy

Most of the time I am very happy, singing, enjoying the beauties (nature, people, ideas) that surround us, processing puns and word play, and thinking about new creative things to do. I carry a small pad of origami paper in my vest and am therefore always ready to fold a gift for a child wherever I am. That makes me happy as well as the kids. Pretty much the only thing I ever fold is the bird with the flapping wings. The kids like to make it fly. I'm currently working on a carry bag for a choir director that will have embroidered music symbols on new pockets on both sides of the bag. I don't do the embroidery, but I know where I can get it done. I will try to deliver this bag without revealing from whom it came. I guess I do want credit for doing that, but only inside myself. That is, I want to proud of myself and what I do. I want to do good things, be nice, be happy. It rubs off.

## 22:46—Crastinate

I'm not a serious logophile, but I do like words, made-up words, pun words, alliteration, rhymes, and love the flow of sleek words like the ones in "High Flight": "Oh, I have slipped the surly bonds of earth and danced the skies on laughter-silvered wings." Wow! This was apparently written by a young pilot who soon gave his life in an aerial dog-fight. I like dialects and reciting poetry in dialect. I only dabble in that, but I really do like it.

So, I came upon the word "procrastinate" (I am very much a procrastinator) and wondered if there were a "concrastinate?" Well, I found out that crastinate is an obsolete word that meant "to put off." Why did they add the "pro?" Words! Gotta love 'em! So I play with words and it gets pretty wild and crazy and non-sensical. Why not?

## 22:47—Self-reliance

Emerson wrote about self-reliance and, as I understand it, it meant to rely on yourself and your inner resources for ideas and strength. My dad frequently mentioned that "if it was too tough for everyone else, it was just right for a Parsons." I followed a lot of that philosophy but was so rigid about it that I didn't ask for help when I should have, like when I was taking an advanced math class and didn't ask for help understanding how to prove a theorem the way the professor wanted us to. For that reason, I never passed that class, so never got my M.A. in Math nor went on to work on a

Ph.D. in math and become a college math teacher, like I had wanted. Even today, I try to rely on myself, and still sometimes push help away when it's offered. It's been one of the things in life that has held me back the most. I don't have all the answers. I never will. And sometimes I "should" ask for help.

I do asks for help frequently, but it's often asking questions via a web browser, not asking a person for help. But I do ask for help when I can't figure out something with IngramSpark, the company I use to publish books for people. Sometimes their processes aren't clear. I ask for help. Yeah!

**22:48 Not My Fault**
This follows a little on sonnet 47, in the sense, that even if you try with all your might, it might not be because you didn't try hard enough. It might actually be because you physically can't do something, that there is something defective or deficient with your physical skills that make it impossible for you to do something. How disappointing to find out after years and years of trying and even getting help, that your physical assets are inadequate to do what you are attempting. I am a good singer, but I can't hear overtones. The audiologist thought it might be because I was a paratrooper and jumped out of planes that had very noisy engines right next to where I jumped out of the plane. Not hearing overtones prevents me from being a better Barbershop singer because that singing requires that in the best quartets, the members, especially the baritone, need to tweak their pitch until they hear the overtone and therefore know the chord is locked in. My ears can't hear those overtones, so I could probably never be a champion barbershop singer. That was a real eye-opener for me. There may be other things that it's not possible for me to do. Of course, I know that some things that I could do at 20 I can do no longer at 82, but the possibilities are still fairly unlimited if I work on something long enough and hard enough.

## 22:49 A Nuff
Sometimes it's good to be silly and then continue to extremes. My sister and I do that. She's two years younger, but we do carry some of the same baggage from our childhood and so can reference some of the quirkiness that came from our parents. I often feel like I'm not up to the task, to the challenge, even though I try hard. I have done some pretty awesome things, I think, but still put myself down because I'm less disciplined that I could be, that I'm out of shape, overweight, and on and on. She tells me that "I Am Enough" and even had that put on a bracelet for me that I wear every day. Of course, here comes the silliness. I am enough becomes I am a nuff. Ah, what is a nuff? How many nuffs does it take to do (something)? Silly! Yep! But her message holds: Just being me is enough, without honors, achievements, values. Just being me is enough.

## 22:50 Self-reliance Uh-Oh
OK, we're revisiting this again; so is that a re-re-visit? This is all about the benefit you give to someone when you let them help you. If we like to help others, then it should not be a surprise that others like to help, and maybe they would like to help me. However, if I am self-reliant then they can't help me. So, I need to remember that sometimes others want to help me, and that's okay, and that doesn't mean I can't be self-reliant.

## 22:51 Gift Gotcha
During the month and half before Christmas, I spent a lot of time, thought and planning pulling together a special gift for the choir director. She is a most amazing woman. She knows what she wants musically, and she knows how to extract that music from the choir. I created a new "masthead" for the choir webpage and thought it would be nice to put the embroidered choir logo on a carry bag for the director. This project kind of took on a life of its own. The project grew and grew and it took over a month to get the logo put into vector format, ordering the main canvas bag, getting material at Joann's for the embroidery patch, creating a second embroidery task, and finally getting the embroidered pockets stitched to the

sides of the canvas bag. Whew! I had a perfect time/place to give the bag but I wanted it to be anonymous so it didn't look like I was trying to brown-nose the director. So the gift was wrapped, placed under the tree at the concert and labeled from Santa.

I know the director got the gift but don't know where it went: did she lose it, did she give it unopened to someone else, was it actually useful? So that got me to thinking, what is the giver of a gift expecting from the recipient? Do we want our gifts appreciated? Yes. But is the greater pleasure in doing all the work to create the gift, to make the gift "happen?"

Will I ever know what happened to that gift? Maybe. Is it important for me to know? Maybe not. Should I have presented the gift separate from the concert and made it clear it was from me? Maybe, yes to both.

I was very proud of the finished bag and what I had gone through to get it made. That is what was important. I did a good job. I need to learn better how to carry through with projects like this.

PS. She uses the gift likes it, and suspected it was from me. I cleared the air, but think I learned something in the process.

## 22:52 Faux Fire

A half dozen or so years ago, my daughter and I built a stage-usable fireplace with logs and a silk flame flickering behind the logs. It was for a Barbershop Chorus Christmas Concert. The fireplace was built with shipping boxes, pop-rivets, and brick-patterned wrapping paper. It can be disassembled into components small enough to fit into a normal sedan. So it can be easily stored and then reassembled next Christmas. It has been used in every Christmas Concert since. It still works. Since that time when the fireplace was built, a chasm sadly has developed between my daughter and me.

Will it always be faux fire, or will it re-kindle sometime in the future? Was the fire during construction faux, or was it real? How does one ever know? It was real from me. And it still is real from me.

www.ingramcontent.com/pod-product-compliance
Lightning Source LLC
Chambersburg PA
CBHW050330120526
44592CB00014B/2131